AN ALBUM OF RECONSTRUCTION

*Illustrated with Pictures from
the William Loren Latz Collection*

AN ALBUM OF RECONSTRUCTION

By William Loren Katz

Franklin Watts, Inc., New York, 1974

Frontispiece: a ruined area of
Charleston, South Carolina.

For My Father

Photographs and prints from the
William Loren Katz Collection.

Library of Congress Cataloging in Publication Data

Katz, William Loren.
    An album of Reconstruction.

    SUMMARY: Discusses the successes, failures, and
collapse of the Reconstruction period.
    Bibliography: p.
    1. Reconstruction–Juvenile literature. [1. Re-
construction] I. Title.
E668.K17   973.8   73–21933
ISBN 0–531–02701–5

CONTENTS

AN ALBUM OF RECONSTRUCTION

INTRODUCTION

Many American historians have called the period of Reconstruction a "tragic era." In their view, the great tragedy was not that it failed, but that it was tried at all. They thought the idea of ex-slaves voting or holding office was foolhardy. In their own way, these historians were as firmly opposed as the Ku Klux Klan to blacks and whites governing the South together.

Until recently this version of Reconstruction has dominated books used in elementary, high school, and college courses. A dishonest story of this period has been told. One school text, for example, says:

> *Foolish laws were passed by the black lawmakers. The public money was wasted terribly and thousands of dollars were stolen straight. Self-respecting Southerners chafed under the horrible regime.*

This book exaggerates some failures and does not mention the contributions of the black-white governments during Reconstruction. It does not tell of their building the public school system in the South, their reform of local governments, prison laws, and tax laws, and their extension of women's rights. The reader is not told that poor whites were allowed to vote for the first time, and that blacks with political power did not discriminate against whites. This is typical of the distortion of Reconstruction history.

Lies about Reconstruction have become a part of American life. Two of America's most famous stories—in book and movie form—were based

As memories of the Civil War and Reconstruction faded, myth began to replace reality. Above: this popular picture of the Civil War era shows a white soldier reading the Emancipation Proclamation to passive but grateful slaves. Entirely forgotten is the fact that black people fought against slavery and thousands of them served in the Union Army helping to win their own emancipation. Below: in the 1915 movie, Birth of a Nation, *history was turned upside-down. Hooded Klansmen were shown saving civilization by driving out black soldiers and officeholders from the South.*

on distortions of this period. The movie *Birth of A Nation* pictured blacks during Reconstruction as evil animals, and made heroes of the Ku Klux Klan. The novel *Gone With the Wind*, later made into a successful movie, carried forward this lie. "The former slaves were now the lords of creation," said the novel, falsely picturing blacks as dominating southern governments at the time.

These lies have helped shape American racial relations. Those who had enslaved black people did not want to believe that they were equal to whites. "How could they help govern a state?" they asked, showing a black who was content under slavery and bewildered by freedom. And if the blacks could not govern themselves or others, then obviously whites had to govern them. It all justified white supremacy and the continued control of black people. That is why the story of Reconstruction has been twisted for so long—it served a useful purpose for certain people.

The myths of Reconstruction are finally beginning to die. Books that tell the true story are beginning to appear. Black and white historians are writing this history the way it really happened: its successes, its failures, and its ultimate collapse.

It has been said that those who ignore history are doomed to repeat it. A correct version of Reconstruction can help us understand our racial problems today in the United States. A true history is vital in providing past information to illuminate present and future problems.

THE CIVIL WAR ENDS

On April 9, 1865, General Lee surrendered to General Grant at Appomattox Courthouse in Virginia. General Lee mounted his horse and rode back to his plantation home. His Confederate soldiers departed for their homes and farms. The northern armies melted away to Ohio, New York, Kansas, and California. Millions of Americans had been under arms and six hundred thousand had died in the four years of battles. But now it was over, and men and women had their dream of peace.

The war had settled some issues, but had created new ones. The defeat of the Confederacy established that states could not leave the Union. It also ended slavery. Although the war was fought over the issue of keeping the Union together or letting it pull apart, slavery had become a central issue as the war progressed. In 1863, to insure Union victory, President Lincoln had announced the emancipation of slaves in land held by the Confederacy. He had also permitted blacks to enter the Union Army. The emancipation policy and the courage of over two hundred thousand black Union soldiers and sailors ended slavery.

Questions of peace, however, were still to be answered. Should Confederate leaders who had waged war against the United States be punished? Should the eleven southern states that had seceded from the Union be permitted to reenter quickly and quietly? Who should decide these questions—Congress or the president? Should the southern states be held as conquered provinces, and ruled by northern troops until they were loyal to the Union again?

Many questions arose regarding the former slaves. They wanted rights and protection for their rights. They and some "radicals" in the North felt blacks were entitled to all the rights of citizens, including the vote. Since ex-slaves had labored so long to build the country without any pay, many wanted land—forty acres and a mule. Many whites in the South and the North wanted to insure that the blacks were still controlled by the whites. How could race relations be settled for four million blacks and approximately twice that number of whites?

LINCOLN AND JOHNSON VIEW RECONSTRUCTION

President Lincoln favored a rapid restoration of the Union. As soon as 10 percent of Southerners in a state stated they were loyal to the Union, the state should be taken back into the Union. He knew there were loyal people in each southern state, and hoped they would be fair to their former slaves. But just a few days after Lee surrendered to Grant, the president was assassinated. He never had an opportunity to put his ideas about southern reconstruction into practice.

Facing page: as this cartoon shows, the battle over Reconstruction pitted those favoring supremacy of the national government against those who held to the doctrine of states' rights. Left: these black soldiers in South Carolina are guarding an old plantation manor that had once controlled their lives—an action symbolic of the enormous changes wrought by the Civil War. In the last years of the Civil War more than 200,000 black soldiers and sailors helped to defeat the Confederacy. In this picture below, the black 55th Massachusetts Regiment marches in triumph through the streets of Charleston, South Carolina. Notice that they are being greeted by the black population but not the white.

Right: Frederick Douglass, the leading black spokesman during Reconstruction, urged Presidents Lincoln and Johnson to grant equality to his people as the only sure way to maintain democracy in the South. Both ignored his advice. To aid the education of ex-slaves, interested whites such as the Board of Trustees of the Peabody Educational Fund (below) provided money for schools and teachers.

Vice-President Andrew Johnson then came to office. A poor white from Tennessee, he hated slavery and slaveowners, and felt they had held back progress in the South. As governor of Tennessee he had opposed secession, and in 1864 he was chosen to run for vice-president with Lincoln.

Where Lincoln was cautious and flexible, Johnson was quick to anger and became unswerving in his views. In the beginning he appeared to favor punishment of Confederates, and a policy insuring that Southerners would not be taken back into the Union until their loyalty had been proven. Johnson also suggested that he might be the "Moses" to lead black people to better times.

President Johnson immediately moved to take the reconstruction of the Confederate states into his own hands. This was the president's job, not Congress's, he argued. He decided to be lenient toward most Confederate leaders but forced the very rich to seek pardons from him personally. As a poor white who was once treated as an inferior by the rich, this may have meant a lot to him.

Throughout Reconstruction President Johnson felt that only he could reconstruct the southern states and accept them back into the Union. He did not wish to share power with Congress, nor did he seek their advice.

CONGRESS VIEWS RECONSTRUCTION

During the war Congress made clear to President Lincoln that it viewed reconstruction of the South as part of its job. Congressmen argued that since the eleven southern states had left the Union, only Congress could readmit them. The Constitution gave Congress power over the admission of new states, and these southern states were now "new."

Congress also reflected the angry mood of many Northerners. Since the Confederates had left the Union and started the war, they deserved punishment. Northern armies had marched into battle singing about the

Confederate president, "We'll hang Jeff Davis to a sour apple tree." Many who had lost sons or fathers wanted revenge.

Increasingly, Congressmen called "radicals" were concerned that a soft policy toward the seceded states would be dangerous to the Union. They warned that loyal men in the South were not safe without troops from the North to protect them. They predicted that Confederate leaders would again rule the region and send Senators and Congressmen back to Washington. Further, they feared that freedom for the blacks would become meaningless if their former masters remained in charge.

The "radicals" in Congress favored a stern policy toward the South. No state should be admitted without Congressional approval. Half of the adult males should be loyal to the Union before acceptance of a state. If necessary, Federal troops should protect loyal whites and ex-slaves in the southern states. Some radicals also thought that key Confederate leaders should face trial for starting the war.

Congress and the president were on a collision course. Their aims and methods were different and neither trusted the other to conduct the delicate job of reconstructing the South.

THE SOUTH IN 1865

Though some of its cities and half of its railroad lines had been destroyed during the war, physical damage in the South was small. Its wealth lay in its soil and this only needed time and work to restore its productivity.

Its few industrial centers had been destroyed, gutted by the Union army. It had no funds to invest in its agriculture. Its one great source of wealth (other than land) was the slaves, and they were free. The eleven defeated Confederate states needed immediate relief for their hungry people and massive economic aid for their factories and fields.

Perhaps most important of all, the southern states were in the midst of a social revolution. Roads were clogged with people on the move—soldiers coming home, civilians returning to their farms and families, blacks searching for relatives separated during slavery. Men, women, and children of both races begged for food, and rummaged through garbage for useful items or something to eat.

FROM SLAVERY
TO FREEDOM

The largest part of the social revolution in the South came from the change in racial relations. Slavery had defined the economic and social relationship of blacks and whites. It not only had made blacks work for whites, but had kept them "in their place." Now it was swept away. Penniless blacks became free laborers. Their former masters were plantation owners without workers. Neither felt much trust in the other, except in rare instances. A new labor system had to replace black bondage.

The position of newly freed blacks among whites was often disturbing. They would no longer submit to being told what to do, to being beaten, to being cared for by whites. As free men and women, they had rights and wished to use them. Many whites reacted to this change with horror, loathing, and fury. Murders of blacks during this time have never been counted, but there were many.

Defeated, the white South was bitter. Anger toward whites loyal to the Union, U.S. Army soldiers, and blacks was daily expressed in towns and throughout the countryside. On the Fourth of July after the war ended, only one group was willing to march in Mobile, Alabama to celebrate American Independence. Six thousand black people, escorted by two black regiments, marched into the main square and heard black speakers praise the United States. The white mayor denounced the celebration and white police began to beat the marchers and arrest them.

To find out about conditions in the South, President Johnson sent Carl Schurz to investigate. A brilliant German immigrant who had served as a Union general, Schurz found race relations bursting into flame everywhere. Colonel Samuel Thomas, in charge of relief in Mississippi and Louisiana, gave Schurz this dismal report:

Wherever I go—the street, the shop, the house, the hotel, or the steamboat—I hear the people talk in such a way as to indicate that they are yet unable to conceive of the negro as possessing any rights at all. Men who are honorable in their dealings with their white neighbors will cheat a negro without feeling a single twinge of their honor. To kill a negro they do not deem murder; to debauch a negro woman they do not think fornication; to take the property away from a negro they do not consider robbery. The people boast that when they get freedmen affairs in their own hands, to use their own classic expression, "the niggers will catch hell."

The reason of all this is simple and manifest. The whites esteem the blacks their property by natural right, and however much they may admit that the individual relations of masters and slaves have been destroyed by the war and by the President's emancipation proclamation, they still have an ingrained feeling that the blacks at large belong to the whites at large, and whenever opportunity serves they treat the colored people just as their profit, caprice or passion may dictate.

Justice from tribunals made up among such people is impossible. Here and there is a fair and just man. . . .

White Southerners' anger toward blacks was aggravated by their dependence on the blacks for labor. "I've never done a day's work in my life," said one Mississippi planter, "and don't know where to start." Colonel Thomas found that blacks "do now, and always have done, all the physical labor of the South." He heard whites speak of "importing labor in the shape of Coolies, Irishmen—anything—to avoid work, any way to keep from putting their own shoulders to the wheel."

Ex-slaves stand outside a store near the Georgia Sea Islands in 1865. Below: liberated early in the war by Union forces, black and white people gather outside a government carpenter's shop in Beaufort, South Carolina.

Above left: this refugee family, uprooted by the Civil War, joins the many others who are clogging southern roads to search for new lives. Below left: long denied the right to worship without a white person present, ex-slaves conducted their own religious services in the woods away from whites. Above: at the edge of a southern waterfront, and in the shadow of buildings scarred by war, ex-slaves sit for a camera perhaps wondering about their uncertain future.

Above: after the Civil War some blacks left the South by ship to go north. Below: both southern and New England women volunteered to help ex-slaves learn useful trades. This scene of the Freedmen's Union Industrial School was sketched in Richmond, Virginia.

BLACKS BEGIN A NEW LIFE

For four million black people, the Civil War meant freedom. First there was shouting and dancing and leaving the plantation. For many, just walking down a road, or being able to decide to do it, was their first exercise in citizenship. Mothers set out to search for daughters and sons who had been sold away during slave days. Children began the long trip back to find their parents. Everywhere blacks were on the move.

There was the basic need to find a job, to make enough money to eat and feed one's family. This was often difficult. Many whites had no money to pay anyone, black or white. Some resented paying blacks for labor they had once received from slaves. Conflict over labor agreements was frequent, with blacks most often the losers. Whites complained that blacks would not work, and blacks complained that whites refused to pay them for their labor.

Some blacks tried hard to make progress. Since their marriages were now recognized by law, many went off to have the formal marriages that were denied them as slaves. Black carpenters began building homes, churches, and schools. Black teachers instructed black children in reading, writing, and arithmetic. In Charleston, one black school used the building that had been a slave auction room. Teachers stood on a platform that had been used to sell other blacks.

THE FREEDMEN'S BUREAU

From the moment of their liberation, black people began the important task of learning how to live as free citizens. In the camps of the advancing bluecoats they took jobs, learned how to read and write, and began to save some money. It was clear that the enormous change required help from the government.

General Oliver O. Howard, who won distinction at Gettysburg's battlefield and marched through Georgia with General Sherman, was summoned to the office of Secretary of War Stanton. He was told an agency was needed to aid the freedmen. "Mr. Stanton held out to me a great basketful of papers saying 'There is your Bureau, General, take it.' I took my bureau and walked out with it." Later General Howard would feel, "I think now that God led me and assigned that work to me."

There had never been in history an organization like the Freedmen's Bureau. It provided relief, gave out land, organized schools, helped make fair labor contracts, and generally tried to help blacks and whites live together in peace. It had power to try cases and make decisions for blacks and whites.

Its greatest work was in the field of education. In five years it spent five million dollars creating 4,329 schools, hiring ten thousand teachers who taught 247,333 pupils. In these schools young and old ex-slaves learned to read and write. "The colored people," reported one visitor in Tennessee in 1865, "are far more zealous in the cause of education than the whites. They will starve themselves, and go without clothes, in order to send their children to school." In one school a visitor observed a family from grandchild to grandmother learning to read and write together. The great black universities of today—Howard, Fisk, Atlanta, Storer, Hampton, and others—began with funds from this government agency.

The least successful part of the Bureau was its effort to distribute land to the freedmen. At the time when western settlers were receiving millions of acres and one hundred million acres were given to western railroads, little land was offered the freedmen. In its entire existence the Bureau gave out only eight hundred thousand acres of southern farms and five thousand pieces of town property. Almost all of this was taken back. When President Johnson granted amnesty to the original Confederate owners who had abandoned their land, he returned it to them.

Throughout its turbulent five years, the Freedmen's Bureau was under constant attack. An effort to renew it was vetoed by the president and then passed over his veto. Violence was often aimed at its schools and officials. In Marianna, Florida, a white mob surrounded the night school and warned the white teacher to close it and leave the county. When the freedmen came to his aid, the mob left. The next time, however, the freedmen were ready and forty came to the school with arms. When the mob arrived again and found the new situation, they rode off and did not come back. Other schools were not as lucky.

The courts established by the Bureau had to decide difficult cases.

Local whites tried to interfere in friendly relationships between blacks and whites, drive off successful black farmers, or force labor contracts on black men and women who could not read them.

Many officials of the Bureau had little understanding or respect for black people, and little sympathy for white Southerners. Some were motivated by a desire to bring religious faith to black and white, believing this was the answer to all problems. Some were out to make money on the southern misery they found. These men complicated a difficult problem. But despite misconceptions and the selfishness of the corrupt officials, the freedmen and the whites in the South were helped by the Bureau, not hindered.

PRESIDENTIAL RECONSTRUCTION

The turmoil in the South was compounded by the conflict in Washington. Against the wishes of Congress, President Johnson proceeded to reconstruct the South his way. He accepted the new state governments formed in Arkansas, Louisiana, Tennessee, and Virginia since they followed his policy of reconstruction. Then he appointed governors in North Carolina, Mississippi, Georgia, Texas, Alabama, South Carolina, and Florida.

These governments were allowed to elect their own leaders if they called a convention to nullify secession, abolish slavery, and not pay the debts of the Confederate government. This they did. The new state governments did not permit blacks to vote and had no black officials.

The president also decided to pardon all Confederates who took an oath of allegiance to the United States. However, one group had to seek his special pardon: officials of the Confederacy who owned $20,000 in property. There was soon a steady stream of important and wealthy Southerners to the White House. By the middle of 1866 the president had granted amnesty to just about everyone.

In the amnesty policy toward white Southerners, their land was returned along with their citizenship. Some of these plantations had been given or sold to ex-slaves by the U.S. Army. General William T. Sherman had given abandoned lands on the South Carolina and Georgia Sea

Islands to those who had been slaves on the vast plantations. Now, the black people were ousted and the lands returned to the white owners. It took U.S. Army officers to calm the angry blacks, who were ready to kill for "our land."

THE CONFEDERATES RIDE AGAIN

With presidential pardons and a policy that left blacks to the care of whites, ex-Confederates again rose to leadership in the South. The eleven southern states soon passed "Black Codes" to regulate blacks, much as "Slave Codes" had controlled slaves. These laws erased whatever dreams of liberty blacks had.

Generally, the Black Codes sought to place black labor under white control again, and to keep black people from equality. Children without parents could be leased to work for a white person. Any black person convicted of vagrancy could be leased out to a white person. This was easy to do since the courts were run by whites. Usually a black man's former owner got first choice of his labor. "This is simply slavery under a new name," said one black. He was right.

The Black Codes prohibited black progress in many other areas. Blacks were forbidden to testify against whites or to bear arms. They could not buy land in certain places, particularly land whites wanted. Black peddlers had to have special licenses to trade in towns, and these cost more money than they could afford. The manufacture and sale of liquor by blacks was halted, since whites wanted control of this profitable business. Several states passed laws segregating public transportation.

In many places blacks held their own meetings to protest the Black Codes. But it did little good, since they could not vote out those who dominated them. However, news of the Black Codes began to stir anger in the North. They indicated to many that the white South had no intention of granting real freedom to the blacks.

A further revelation of Confederate power came in the first southern elections after the war. To the 39th Congress Southerners elected nine Confederate army officers, six cabinet officers, fifty-eight Congressmen, and Confederate Vice-President Alexander H. Stephens.

Left: the right of black people to a formal, legal marriage was one of the most important rights they won with the defeat of slavery. Even before the guns of the Civil War had been silenced, blacks were teaching each other to read and write. This scene below of the Zion School was sketched in a Charleston, South Carolina room, formerly used as an auction hall for selling slaves.

Above: this home for orphaned children was run by and for blacks in Memphis, Tennessee. Above right: in Memphis, the Freedmen's Bureau office tried to help with many problems that arose from blacks and whites dealing with each other on a level of equality. Below right: this political cartoon of the day presents the Freedmen's Bureau as a governmental officer trying to keep the peace between angry whites and blacks.

Left: typical of the many New England school teachers who came south to teach the freed blacks was Laura M. Towne, photographed with three of her pupils in 1866. The educational efforts of the Freedmen's Bureau is dramatically shown in this photograph above, taken at Freedmen's Village in Arlington, Virginia, as a huge class of black children and adults stand outside holding their school books. Immediately after the Civil War there were murders and persecutions of those southern whites who had aided or been sympathetic to the Union cause. Below is an artist's conception of the murder of Senator Case of Tennessee by a rebel guerilla.

CONGRESS CHALLENGES THE PRESIDENT

If the return of Confederate power or the Black Codes did not bother President Johnson, they disturbed Congress. Led by Congressman Thaddeus Stevens in the House of Representatives and Senator Charles Sumner in the Senate, the "radicals" decided to take control of Reconstruction from the president.

Though the heart of their program was granting the vote to southern blacks, their basic aim was not to help blacks. The Republican Congress felt that President Johnson had allowed the Union victory on the battlefield to slip away in peacetime. To insure loyalty in the South, they felt it necessary to crush again the power they had defeated on the battlefields—the southern aristocracy. And to keep the South loyal, they needed black suffrage.

The Republicans wanted the South in the hands of Republicans, and were willing to use black help to gain this. After all, blacks had been freed in a war waged by a Republican administration and president. They would assuredly vote Republican, especially if Republicans gave them the vote.

Congress refused to seat any Representatives or Senators from the South until it had admitted the state they were from. Next, Congress passed a Civil Rights Act granting blacks citizenship and equal rights. This was designed to end the Black Codes. President Johnson vetoed it, but Congress passed it over his veto. Congress then formed a Committee of fifteen to run Reconstruction.

The Committee of fifteen proposed a new Constitutional amendment to protect black rights. This Fourteenth Amendment also granted equal rights to ex-slaves, and prohibited states from denying them under any pretext. President Johnson urged states not to ratify it, but it was ratified by 1868. Repeatedly Congress would pass laws on Reconstruction and President Johnson would veto them. Then Congress would pass them over his veto.

DEFEAT OF THE PRESIDENT

The battle between Congress and the president echoed in the South. Those who favored the Congressional approach tried to rally blacks and whites in Loyal Leagues or Republican clubs. Those who wished to keep control in white hands, as did President Johnson, tried to halt Republican growth. Many whites felt the issue was their supremacy over blacks. They saw Republicanism as granting blacks power over whites.

Violence exploded first in Memphis, Tennessee. In three days of rioting, whites attacked blacks and killed forty-seven. Only one white was injured. The white mob destroyed ninety homes, twelve schools, and four churches—properties that demonstrated black progress.

Another riot struck New Orleans that same summer of 1866. The city was a cosmopolitan center where French, Spanish, Africans, and Americans had produced a racially mixed population with a rich culture of music and literature. A group of black men assembled for a political meeting at the Mechanics Institute. The mayor, a member of a secret society called the Southern Cross, had his heavily armed police surround the hall. A minor incident led to a police assault that killed almost fifty people.

General Philip Sheridan, military commander of Louisiana, surveyed the death scene and investigated the event. He came to a simple conclusion: "It was no riot. It was an absolute massacre by the police . . . a murder which the mayor and police perpetrated without the shadow of necessity."

By now President Johnson and Congress were actively seeking the total defeat of one another. They both focused on the Congressional elections of that November, 1866. President Johnson toured the nation blaming the racial violence in Memphis and New Orleans on Congressman Stevens and Senator Sumner. He screamed and cursed his enemies, shocking his audiences, and some newspapers thought he might be drunk. Republican Congressmen urged voters to elect more, not fewer, Radicals, and President Johnson was resoundingly defeated.

CONGRESS TAKES CONTROL

After their victory over President Johnson at the polls, more Radicals gathered in Congress. They prepared to seize control of Reconstruction from the president. By March of 1867, they passed a law regulating the Reconstruction of the former Confederate states. Congress's new program divided the defeated states into five military districts and then sent U.S. troops into them.

To return to the Union, each southern state had to follow certain rules. First, it had to call a new constitutional convention to rewrite its basic laws. All adult men, white and black, were eligible to vote for delegates. Second, the new governments set up by the constitutions had to guarantee black voting rights and ratify the Fourteenth Amendment to the U.S. Constitution. Third, the ex-Confederate leaders were denied the right to vote or hold office.

President Johnson vetoed this new law since its provisions swept away his control of Reconstruction. Congress quickly passed it again over his veto. Then Congress went even further. Originally they thought that a majority of eligible voters in a state should pass on their new constitution. But they changed this to a majority of those actually voting on the new constitution. This prevented opponents of a new constitution from defeating it by simply refusing to vote.

Troops were sent south to carry out the Radical program. A vast social revolution was under way where slavery had once ruled. In five southern states—Alabama, Florida, Mississippi, Louisiana, and South Carolina—more blacks than whites registered to vote. Those whites who registered with the blacks were called "scalawags" or traitors by their enemies.

In the turmoil of change many Northerners came south seeking either to help or to make their fortune. They were called "carpetbaggers" by resentful Southerners.

IMPEACHMENT OF A PRESIDENT

The same day Congress passed its first reconstruction act, it passed another law, the Tenure of Office Act. Both were designed to ensure that Congress controlled Reconstruction. But the second law was specifically aimed at President Johnson and was meant to keep him from interfering with Congress's plans. It forbade him to remove a cabinet member from office without consent of the Senate. Congress wanted to be certain the president did not replace Secretary of War Stanton, the only man in the presidential cabinet who favored their radical plans.

In the next year, as the president continued to veto reconstruction acts of Congress, there were demands from Radicals for his impeachment. They had no legal case, only their own anger at his repeated use of power to hold back their plans. Nevertheless, they demanded his impeachment. President Johnson then fired Secretary of War Stanton and replaced him with a general. He felt the Tenure of Office Act was unconstitutional and that it should be tested in the courts.

But Congress now thought it had an issue that justified impeachment. Each branch of the government plays a special role in impeachment. The House of Representatives acts as prosecutor. The Chief Justice of the United States acts as judge. And the Senate votes as a jury. To remove the president, two-thirds of those Senators present must vote a guilty verdict.

The legal arguments for and against the president rang in the halls of Congress. But those who impeached him could not make a strong case that he was guilty of "high crimes." In May, 1868, the Senate voted thirty-five guilty and nineteen not guilty votes, one less than the necessary two-thirds votes to convict him. By a single Senate vote, Johnson remained president of the United States. But his career in office and politics was almost over. And although he was not removed from the presidency, his power was drastically cut.

Congressman Thaddeus Stevens (far right) and Senator Charles Sumner (right) led those who sought to wrest control of Reconstruction from the hands of President Johnson. Below: this political cartoon of the day shows President Andrew Johnson and Congressman Thaddeus Stevens as engineers whose trains are on a collision course.

*Above: blacks in Memphis
fleeing white rioters.
Left: Memphis rioters
burning a school house
used by the freedmen.*

In this cartoon above, President Johnson is shown as a wicked Iago telling a black veteran that he is his friend while in the background, blacks are being murdered during the Memphis and New Orleans riots. Right: in Charleston, South Carolina blacks and whites engage in a street riot. Eruptions of street fighting in the South mirrored the conflict between the president and Congress in Washington. President Andrew Johnson is pictured in this cartoon on the facing page as Samson tearing down the temple of Reconstruction by his firing of Secretary of War Stanton.

In this cartoon above, a resentful President Johnson and an equally resentful former Confederate leader are shown sneering at the thought that a black man would be allowed to vote. Right: Secretary of War Edwin M. Stanton. Above right: so many people wanted to see President Johnson's trial for impeachment that tickets were issued. As the Senate considered impeachment, stories continued to come in from the South telling of the murder and mistreatment of those who were loyal to the Union or to blacks. This political cartoon on the facing page is based on an incident in Charleston, South Carolina when the fire brigade refused to carry an American flag in a local parade and instead carried a large portrait of Confederate General Stonewall Jackson.

U.S. SENATE
Impeachment of the President
ADMIT THE BEARER
MARCH 13 - 1868

Geo. T. Brown
Sergeant-at-Arms.

Philp & Solomons. Wash. D.C.

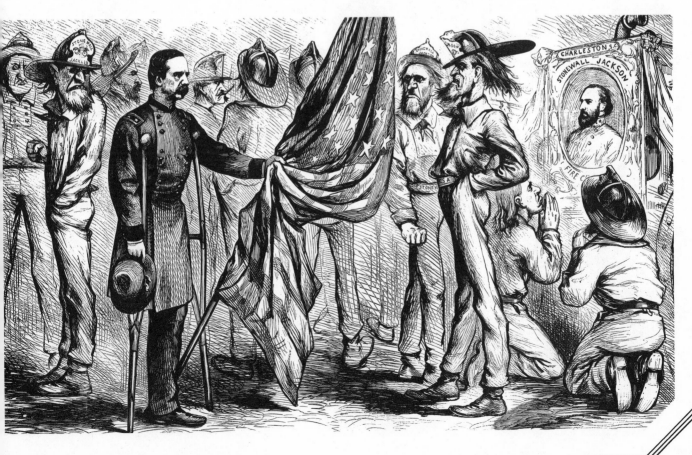

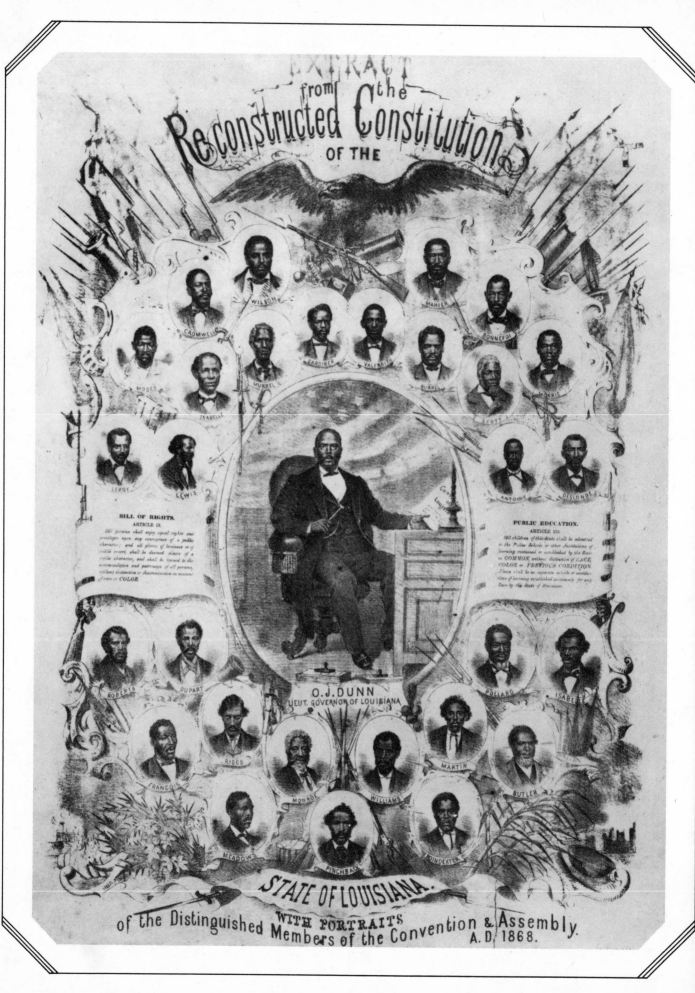

REWRITING SOUTHERN CONSTITUTIONS

Under the protection of federal troops, black and white voters elected delegates to conventions that would write new constitutions for their states. Although black voters formed a majority in five states, only in South Carolina did black delegates outnumber whites. In Louisiana there were an equal number, forty-nine of each. Mississippi sent only sixteen blacks of the one hundred delegates, and most states did about the same. Black voters were more than willing to elect whites they considered trustworthy.

From the beginning, convention delegates made great efforts to co-operate on democratic constitutions. Blacks stated that they wanted only equality as citizens, not "social equality." Many whites tried hard to work as equals among people whom they had only known as slaves. But for some whites, these whites working with blacks were scalawags betraying their state by uniting with blacks. "Barbarism," shouted one white, "is overwhelming civilization by physical force. It is the slave rioting in the halls of his master, and putting that master under his feet."

The new state constitutions were far from radical. They granted equal political rights to black and white alike. Written as they were by poor or lower class delegates, they gave more attention to the problems of the poor than ever before in the South. Many official positions that were once appointed became open to election. Taxes were made fairer for the poor. Prison reforms abolished whipping inmates and jailing a man for debt. A large number of crimes punishable by death were reduced to prison terms. State homes for the handicapped and hospitals for the ill and the insane

Left: black members of the Louisiana constitutional convention of 1868.

were improved. Women were given more rights than ever before in the South.

One of the great contributions of these conventions and the governments that followed was their work in education. Before the war, schooling had been a privilege of the rich. The poor were excluded. The black and white delegates remedied this by providing for public education. The poor felt education meant power, and was as important as citizenship.

In South Carolina where black delegates outnumbered whites seventy-six to forty-eight, the new constitution brought democracy to the heart of the old Confederacy. Property qualifications for voting or holding office were abolished. Now a poor man without any property could vote for and be elected to any office in the state. City and county governments were modernized. But above all else, the new constitution promised "universal education" open to black and white alike. In South Carolina where blacks dominated the convention, there was little to criticize in the constitution they drew up. Some papers called it "the maddest, most unscrupulous, and infamous revolution in history." But it was also the most democratic.

Rather than trying to dominate the South, blacks had shown an interest in doing their part and learning how to govern. An ex-slave named Nash in South Carolina told the other delegates, "I believe, my friends, and fellow citizens, we are not prepared for this suffrage. But we can learn. Give a man tools and let him commence to use them, and in time he will learn a trade. So it is with voting. We may not understand it at the start, but in time we shall learn to do our duty."

So great was the thirst for education that black delegates did not demand school integration. They felt integrated schools would so antagonize whites that the funds for education would never be voted. Southern schools remained segregated throughout Reconstruction. Only at the University of South Carolina and in the New Orleans public schools did blacks and whites study together. This experiment continued for a half dozen years, and drew little resistance from whites. "The children were simply kind to each other in the schoolroom as in the streets and elsewhere," reported the state commissioner of education in Louisiana in 1874.

A NEW DAY
DAWNS IN
THE SOUTH

New governments were elected in the southern states following the constitutional conventions. Again, black men played a part, but not a dominating one, in each state. In South Carolina black members outnumbered whites in the lower house of the legislature, but whites still dominated the governorship, supreme court, and state senate. In all other states blacks were a minority in each part of the government.

Black men and women sought jobs, homes, and education along with their new rights. There were black school principals, sheriffs, mayors, and state officials. There was a black mayor of Natchez, Mississippi, a black governor (for forty-three days) in Louisiana, a black superintendent of schools in Florida, and black legislators in Texas. Black army units patrolled southern urban and rural areas, helping to keep the peace.

From the beginning, some whites waited for the moment to restore white supremacy. As soon as the new Georgia legislature met in 1868, its whites voted to expel its twenty-seven elected black members. One black member, Henry M. Turner, lectured the white legislators for hours on his rights. "I am here to demand my rights, and to hurl thunderbolts at the men who would dare to cross the threshold of my manhood." Reverend Turner and the others were later reinstated.

Many blacks waged a long battle to win their rights to public transportation and accommodation. After a public meeting in Charleston, South Carolina, blacks tested their right to ride the streetcars. Whites were upset, blacks were asked to leave the cars, and some conductors unhitched the horses and left the cars standing. In other places troops had to restore order.

In Louisville, Kentucky, 1872, a black teen-ager began his own sit-in on a horse-drawn streetcar. This time white teen-agers dragged him from the car. When he fought back, white police arrested him. Soon other young blacks took up the campaign, sitting stony and silent when asked to leave. After the conductors left in anger, the young blacks ran the cars, stopping at each stop for passengers. Finally, the company agreed to allow blacks to ride their streetcars.

At the University of South Carolina, a revolution in education was taking place. Blacks were admitted as students and as faculty members. The black secretary of state became the first of his race to enter the university. Some whites immediately left. Prominent in the classes of the law school were members of the state legislature. A white visitor from the North reported, "I was informed that dozens of members were occupied every spare moment outside of the sessions [of the legislature] in faithful study."

Slowly but surely, poor blacks and whites were securing more land of their own. Sometimes in cooperative ventures, they bought land and built farms and homes. Above all else, the average Southerner, black or white, was a farmer who wanted some land of his own. Efforts by Congress or state legislatures to provide cheap land failed. The ex-slave's dream of "forty acres and a mule" remained a dream. It would have meant transferring land owned by wealthy whites to poor whites and blacks. Only a few dared to advocate this radical proposal.

Perhaps the greatest change took place among the common people. For the first time in their lives, many felt they had a place in their state. They could vote for their leaders and thus have a say in laws and taxes. They could attend school if they could spare the time from work. They no longer lived under the shadow of the slaveowner. But this democracy depended upon cooperation between whites who had always been told they were superior, and black people who had always been told they were inferior. How long would it hold up?

With passage of the Civil Rights Act by Congress and ratification of the Fourteenth Amendment guaranteeing equality of treatment, Reconstruction was taken out of the hands of the president and blacks were given the rights of citizens. Below: a northern artist touring the South sketched these black and white South Carolina legislators.

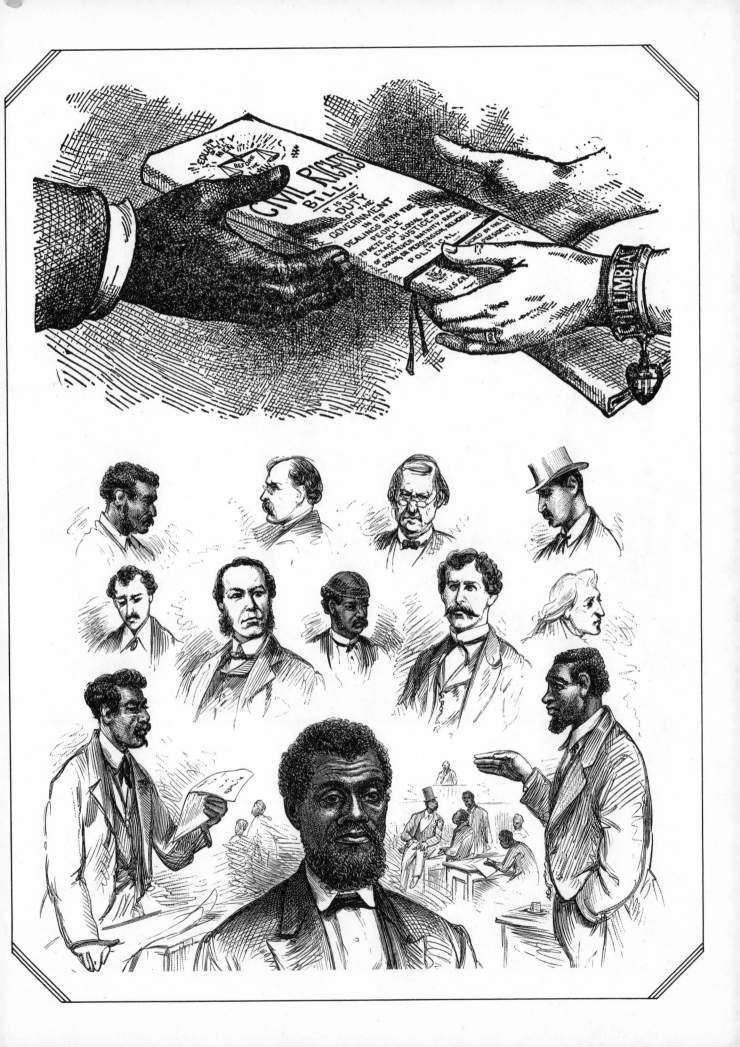

Left: *quick to assert their newly won power, blacks rallied in the South in support of the Union and their own candidates. Above: for the first time in history, blacks were able to vote in many southern states.*

Right: P. B. S. Pinchback, a black man, served as Lieutenant Governor of Louisiana and for forty-three days as Governor of the state. Below: this was the first mixed jury in Washington, D.C. On facing page: blacks played a prominent part in the South Carolina legislature during the early 1870's.

THE NORTH
DURING
RECONSTRUCTION

The North was of two minds during Reconstruction. Part of it wanted the rebels punished, liberty insured for the blacks, and the Republican party fastened on the South forever. But another group simply wanted peace in the South, felt uneasy about aiding blacks against whites, and looked forward to doing business again with the men who had been the South's old aristocracy and slaveowners.

It was an age of enormous industrial expansion in which businessmen used both legal and illegal means of getting ahead. The strong were considered better. The weak and unfortunate were usually regarded with contempt. In the rush for money, fewer and fewer people in the North remained concerned about either the ex-slaves or the poor whites of the South.

In 1868 Ulysses S. Grant was elected president, winning with the votes of blacks in several key southern states. Though he was innocent, his administration was mired in corruption. Members of his cabinet were guilty of stealing public monies. Two financial cheats, Jay Gould and James Fisk, captured the gold market with aid from some government officials and made a fortune. The secretary of war was impeached for taking bribes from those who wanted to set up trading posts in the Indian Territory. One of President Grant's secretaries was involved in a "Whiskey Ring" which stole federal tax monies. Important Congressmen were charged with accepting stock for a company that did business with the government, and two were censured for misconduct. In the 1873 "salary grab" the president and Congress doubled their salaries, but public anger forced the Congress to repeal its increase.

By 1873 an overexpansion of industries and railroads led to a business depression. Called the "panic of 1873," it led to unemployment and fear of further depressions. In the rush for money, firms went out of business. People were suddenly thrown out of work. Families worried about how they would pay their bills. In many places mothers and teen-agers had to find work so they could help their families survive.

CORRUPTION
IN THE
SOUTH

Like the rest of the nation, the southern governments had their share of corrupt and dishonest officials during this time of easy money. Whites and blacks, ex-Confederates and ex-Yankees, former plantation owners, and poor mechanics fell victim to the "big chance" to make some dishonest money.

Enemies of the new black-white governments blamed corruption entirely on black officeholders. They charged that all corruption stemmed from ex-slaves and their carpetbagger and scalawag friends. It was true that some blacks, carpetbaggers, and scalawags were among those "in on the take." But so were many other Southerners.

Most of the money taken illegally from governments at this time went to railroads owned by rich whites. Through a variety of dishonest schemes, they defrauded the government of millions of dollars in funds and land. Blacks and poor whites could steal only the leavings of the rich.

The corruption that took place in the Reconstruction governments was similar to that in other places. Blacks benefited least since whites had had more experience in dishonest government. When the black-white governments were replaced by all-white ones, the corruption did not stop; sometimes it increased. In the North during this time, the Tammany Hall political organization stole more money from New York City than all the Reconstruction governments combined—$100,000,000. Its infamous Tweed Ring ran the city governments for its own profit. Many ended up in jail, including Boss Tweed, and others fled to Europe.

Reconstruction governments were repeatedly charged with excessive corruption. Those who never believed blacks could govern themselves assumed they must be the cause of corruption.

To convince everyone that blacks needed whites to control them, this myth was spread by white supremacists. Stories of "black corruption" were blown up out of proportion and circulated throughout the nation. For a hundred years school texts continued to teach these lies and exaggerations.

THE
KU KLUX
KLAN

═══════

Soon after the war ended, a group of whites formed an organization to aid widows and orphans of the Confederate cause. It was called the Ku Klux Klan. In a short time it changed its purpose to oppose black freedom. Its members were pledged by secret oaths to uphold the life of the Old South—meaning white supremacy. Soon the Klan attacked ex-slaves, carpetbaggers, and scalawags.

The Klan's aim was the restoration of white control over blacks. It tried to rid the region of all who opposed this purpose. Teachers were tarred and feathered, schools and churches bombed, and white and black officeholders driven out. Klansmen rode at night, dressed in white gowns and hoods, first trying to frighten away enemies, then using violence if this did not work.

They spared neither men, women, nor children. Often their targets were successful black farmers and businessmen since this class destroyed the lie of black inferiority. Klan riders also struck at the Republican party, hoping to drive it from the South since it offered blacks a political home.

It proved impossible to suppress the Klan entirely. The U.S. Army had sent only twenty-five thousand of its sixty thousand soldiers to southern states. Most of these were assigned to guarding the Texas border separating Mexico and the United States. Because the Klansmen struck at night and were protected by important men in the state, they were rarely punished. Colonel George W. Kirk of the U.S. Army in North Carolina reported:

> *The juries were made up of Ku-Klux, and it was impossible for any of the loyal people to get justice before the courts. Not less than fifty or sixty persons have been killed by the Ku-Klux in the State, besides some three or four hundred whippings, and there has never been a man convicted that I have heard of. . . . Colored men cannot get justice, cannot get their hard earned money.*

BLACK CONGRESSMEN ARE ELECTED

By 1870 the Fifteenth Amendment was ratified, giving federal protection to black voters. That same year the first black man to sit in the U.S. Congress was elected from the South. Between 1870 and 1901, twenty-two black Congressmen would take their places in the House of Representatives or Senate.

Half of these men were ex-slaves, and all were honest lawmakers, interested in representing the people of their district. James G. Blaine, Republican presidential candidate, who served with them, said of their abilities:

The colored men who took seats in both the Senate and House did not appear ignorant or helpless. They were as a rule studious, earnest, ambitious men whose public conduct . . . would be honorable to any race.

Half of the black Congressmen had attended college, and many were forceful orators. Congressman Robert Smalls was the war hero who had sailed the battleship *Planter* out of Charleston Harbor and delivered it to the Union Navy. All were loyal Republicans who tried to bring progress to whites and blacks alike. "I am true to my own race," said one black Congressman, "but at the same time, I would not have anything done which would harm the white race."

Black Congressmen spoke for many reforms. Besides advocating civil rights laws, they wanted federal aid for education. Senator B. K. Bruce of Mississippi, the only full-term black Senator, urged fair treatment for American Indians and Asian immigrants. In the 1880s these were not popular causes.

In and out of Congress, black Congressmen spoke against discrimination from personal experience. Jefferson Long of Georgia had to hide on his election day and seven of his followers were shot by a mob. John R. Lynch of Mississippi told his fellow Congressmen of how he was forced to ride in inferior train cars for blacks to Washington.

The era of Reconstruction was marked in the North and the South by political corruption. This cartoon of the day pictures U.S. senators as wild beasts fighting over the spoils of office. Above right: throughout the Reconstruction period blacks met in northern and southern state conventions to demand equality of treatment and the right to vote. Below right: after the Civil War the Supreme Court granted admission to John H. Rock, the first black lawyer, to present a case before the high judicial body.

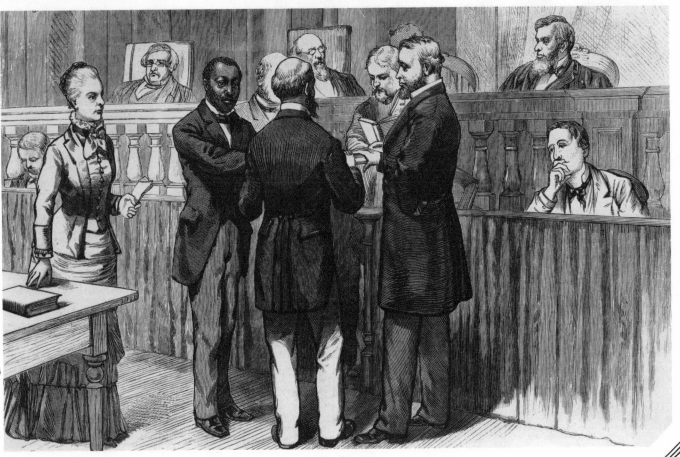

On facing page: this political cartoon of 1874 blames southern black legislators for corruption in South Carolina. The caricature of the black man reflects the rise of anti-black feelings throughout the South. Above: this cartoon purports to show a scene in the South Carolina legislature as blacks eat, drink, and enjoy themselves rather than attend to business. Left: wearing white masks and carrying guns and knives, the Ku Klux Klan sought to terrorize its enemies into silence. They struck against blacks and those whites who tried to help them.

THE WHIPPING-POST.
HUNTED DOWN WITH BLOOD-HOUNDS.
SLAVERY FOR YEARS.
BRANDED AND MAN-ACLED.
THE AUCTION BLOCK—HUSBAND AND WIFE, PARENT AND CHILD, BRO-THER AND SISTER SOLD APART.
DAUGHTERS, MOTHERS, WIVES, AND SIS-TERS RUINED.
KNOWLEDGE A SEALED BOOK.
FORT PILLOW MASSACRE.
"Resolved by the Congress of the Confederate States of America, That the thanks of Congress are due and are hereby cordially tendered to Major-General Forrest and other officers and men of his command, for their late brilliant and successful campaign in Mississippi, West Tennessee, and Kentucky—a campaign which has conferred on its authors fame as enduring as the records of the struggle which they have so brilliantly illustrated."
NO QUARTER TO THE "NIGGER!"
NEW YORK RIOTS—BURNING OF THE COLORED ORPHAN ASYLUM; LAMP-POST GALLOWS.
HOMES BURNED.
NEW ORLEANS AND MEMPHIS MASSACRES.
"A NEGRO HAS NO RIGHTS WHICH A WHITE MAN IS BOUND TO RESPECT."
"THIS IS A WHITE MAN'S GOVERNMENT."
"The nigger and the white man are not likely to agree, unless the nigger yields to the white man's views, which he can do, or die."—The Jefferson (Texas).
"We must make the negro understand we are the men we were when we held them in abject bondage."—Meridian (Miss.) Mercury.
"Agree among yourselves, and act firmly on this agreement, that you will not employ any one who votes the Radical ticket."—WADE HAMPTON.
"And now I say that, unless the negroes submit to the intelligent guidance of the powerful white race, their fate will be that of the Indians: they will be exterminated. The negroes can only be happy and prosperous as long as they are guided by the intelligence of the white race. Whenever it is sought to disfranchise the intelligence of the country, and make it subordinate to the ignorance of the country; whenever it is sought to subordinate the white race of the country to the black barbarism of the negro, the prosperity of the country is at an end."—BLAIR.
"We are bound to have a war of races, and when there is one drop of blood spilled, we predict that it will flow as freely as does the Mississippi."—The Jefferson (Texas).

BULLETS—REBEL PROTESTS AGAINST RE-PUBLICAN MEETINGS; CAMILLA, GEOR-GIA. KU-KLUX KLAN.
NEGRO KILLED—"ONE VOTE LESS."—Rich-mond Whig.
EXPULSION OF COLORED MEMBERS OF THE HOUSE OF REPRESENTATIVES IN GEORGIA.
EXPELLED FROM THE JURY BOX.
FORCED AWAY FROM THE POLLS.

BURNING SCHOOL-HOUSES AND CHURCH-ES THROUGHOUT THE "RECONSTRUCT-ED STATES."
HUNG UP OR SHOT DOWN IN THE ROADS AND STREETS.
"COLORED CRIMINALS SUFFER SEVERER PUNISHMENT THAN WHITES GUILTY OF THE SAME CRIMES."
THE GEORGIA MASSACRE.
"WE DESPISE THE NEGRO."—N. Y. World.

This political cartoon on the facing page shows the long history of anti-black violence in the South. The Ku Klux Klan notice above was intended to frighten off its enemies and was presented as evidence before a congressional committe investigating the Klan. At top: Currier and Ives, the famous American lithographers, produced this picture of the first seven blacks to enter the U.S. Congress. Left: ex-slave Robert Smalls represented South Carolina five times in the U.S. Congress.

Left: this famous cartoon by Thomas Nast shows a bitter Jefferson Davis cursing Senator Hiram Revels of Mississippi, a black man who took Davis's old seat in the U.S. Senate. Above: Congressman Robert B. Elliott of South Carolina rose to challenge former Confederate Vice-President Alexander H. Stephens for opposing the 1875 Civil Rights Bill.

THE "MISSISSIPPI PLAN"

By 1870 violence had grown to enormous proportions in the South. In Virginia, North Carolina, Tennessee, and Georgia, black-white governments had been forced out of office, often at gun point. Klan murders had driven off black and white politicians, carpetbaggers, and scalawags. In 1871 Congress ordered an investigation of the Ku Klux Klan, the White Camelia, the Pale Faces, the White Brotherhood, the 76 Association, and other organizations bent on ending black political power and the Republican party.

In thirteen volumes of testimony Congress established that these organizations had directed a massive reign of terror. New laws were passed to suppress the Klan, and for a time the violence lessened.

By now many in the North were disgusted with the continuation of southern racial conflict. Northern whites talked of "home rule" for the South. This meant removing the federal troops and turning over the state governments to whites. Many leading business publications in the North supported this idea. White rule, they reasoned, would end violence and business would prosper again.

In the election of 1875, whites in Mississippi openly announced a new "shotgun" policy. They proposed to use any threat or force to win the election from the black-white government that ruled the state. Democrats organized white militia companies that drilled and paraded through black

This cartoon shows how important federal forces were in protecting the black man from his enemies in the South.

regions. Republican and black meetings were broken up and their crowds forced to listen to Democratic speakers. Riots were provoked with blacks and innocent voters massacred. By election day thousands of blacks and their white supporters were hiding instead of voting. White supremacy carried Mississippi by force in 1875 and set a pattern to be followed elsewhere.

ECONOMIC THREATS

To overturn Reconstruction, whites employed more than violence. In some cases Republicans and blacks could not buy at white stores. Laborers were asked to sign contracts with their bosses that forbade their joining "Loyal Leagues" or the Republican party. Lists of Republican voters were printed in newspapers and these people soon found their crops set ablaze, their children abused, their wives insulted.

Republican power in the South rested on weak foundations. First, the troops were too few and too busy to halt the growing white violence toward the Reconstruction governments and their leaders. Power that rested so firmly on outside troops could not last. Secondly, governments established by black and white Southerners had political but not economic power. The poor still labored in the South on the fields of the rich. They could be fired any time—and were fired at election time if they voted Republican.

Most blacks became part of the sharecropping system. This meant they labored for whites on land they did not own. In return for using white land and tools, the blacks had to pay with a portion of the crop—from one-half to two-thirds. All records were kept by the landlord. Usually the sharecroppers could not even read those records. Very often they were informed at the end of each year that each owed more money than he made.

The sharecropping system became a new form of slavery, one that kept the black man from power and independence. Unable to raise himself economically, neither was he free to vote as he pleased. Power increasingly moved into the hands of enemies of equality. Those blacks who had their own land were often the targets of night raiders.

THE ELECTION OF 1876

By the end of Grant's second term as president, Northerners were tired of hearing about violence and corruption in the South. The presidential election of 1876 pitted Rutherford B. Hayes, Republican, against Samuel J. Tilden, the Democratic candidate. Southern violence was commonplace in the election. The "Red Shirt" campaign of South Carolina brought out hundreds of horsemen to terrorize Republican voters.

The election for president was close and South Carolina, Florida, and Louisiana—states that still had Reconstruction governments—held the key. It was unclear who won the election since there was so much violence. A special committee was set up by Congress to examine the election results in those three states and determine whether Hayes or Tilden had won. To win, Hayes needed all three states on his side.

A compromise between northern and southern states was arranged. It gave the presidency to Hayes. But Southerners demanding "home rule" also won. In return for their accepting his election, Hayes promised to withdraw all federal troops from the South. This meant that the last regions under federal supervision—South Carolina, Florida, and Louisiana—would again be ruled by those believing in white supremacy.

From this point on, the North left the governments of the South alone. There was little talk of black rights, only of the burden it was to protect them. The "better class" of Southerners, many argued, would protect the blacks anyway.

Northern interest in the South centered on business. Not black rights, but profitable trading with southern states mattered to northern manufacturers. Principles of justice took second or last place to economic gain. Had the Northerners—a majority of them—really favored equality with blacks? Their own record says no. Their own future dealings with northern blacks say no.

This cartoon at left shows how ineffective federal forces were in protecting blacks from their enemies in the South. Blacks often organized to resist those who tried to drive them from office or crush their rights. On the facing page these blacks in Louisiana set up barricades outside a court house but were finally massacred after a three-hour battle. As anti-black violence mounted in the South, many felt they had no choice but to bear arms or to flee. These black men and women below are hiding in the swamps of Louisiana.

A conservative and deeply religious people, rural whites in the South resented and resisted change of any kind. The people above are from North Carolina, and at right from Georgia. Southern novelists such as Thomas Dixon pictured the old Confederates as heroes facing the evil of black rule. This print at top of facing page is from his novel, The Leopard's Spots. At bottom of facing page: wealth and eventually power would remain in the hands of those families who had been prominent in the South during slavery.

Above: as violence over Reconstruction mounted in the South, Horace Greeley organized liberal Republicans opposed to the policy of using federal troops to preserve the peace. This political cartoon at right shows Horace Greeley trying to hide all efforts to deny equality to blacks.

In this political cartoon above, President Grant is pictured as a knight engaged in battle. This campaign poster at right shows the Republican contestants in the 1876 presidential race.

With the restoration of white supremacy, those blacks and their white allies who had been members of the South Carolina legislature during Reconstruction were either driven from office, slain, or forced to flee the state.

RETURN OF
WHITE SUPREMACY

The restoration of white rule in the South marked another era of aristo-cratic control. For black Americans it was the low point in their lives as free American men and women. The future was in the hands of their enemies, those who only sought to exploit their labor.

In 1879 a vast migration of southern blacks left for Kansas. It was based on the knowledge that black rights in the South counted for nothing among whites. Said Henry Adams, an ex-slave from Georgia and one of the leaders of this exodus, "we lost all hopes. . . . We said that the whole South—every state in the South—had got into the hands of the very men that held us as slaves [who] were holding the reins of government over our heads in every respect almost, even the constable up to the governor."

Committees met and dispatched investigators to check on conditions throughout the South. Free men, they discovered, "were still being whipped, some of them by the old owners." Appeals to the president and the Senate brought no response. Neither did a request for funds for a migration to Africa, nor appeals to foreign governments for aid. Within one year twenty thousand to forty thousand blacks migrated from the South to the West.

Whites were frightened. Southerners blocked Mississippi River travel of blacks, and threatened to jail or fine those who encouraged the exodus of their laborers. President Hayes was told, "every river landing is block-aded by white enemies of the colored exodus; some of whom are mounted and armed, as if we are at war." Congress ordered an investigation. Demo-crats were convinced it was a plot to move voteless southern blacks to states where they could and would vote Republican.

The "Exodus of 1879" was not a conspiracy; it was an effort by south-ern blacks to escape the terror and hate of white supremacy. During this time a few black legislators were elected to state legislatures in Louisiana, Georgia, and South Carolina.

Reconstruction had proved that blacks were capable of running a government. It had proved men of both races could do this together. This became the buried meaning of Reconstruction, for these truths were denied a place in history books. Those who sought to justify segregation and discrimination wanted no accounts of black accomplishments, successful laws, administrations, and reforms in the South. Instead, they told a different tale in books, plays, and movies.

Movies such as *Birth of a Nation* and *Gone with the Wind* made heroes of the Ku Klux Klan and denied the black contribution to southern Reconstruction. The success of the school system that poor black and white legislators had voted for was hidden. Rarely mentioned were the black Congressmen, sheriffs, mayors, judges, and school superintendents who tried mightily to build a new South free of prejudice and ignorance.

RECONSTRUCTION BALANCE SHEET

From 1868 to 1895 the constitution of South Carolina drawn up by seventy-six blacks and forty-eight whites remained the law of the state. The constitution drawn up by a majority of blacks remained in effect even though the state was in the hands of those who believed in black inferiority: proof of the value of the work of the Reconstruction legislators.

In 1895 South Carolina called a new convention to rewrite the 1868 constitution. One of the delegates was Thomas E. Miller, a former black Congressman. He told the white delegates that many laws passed by the black-white government still "stand as living witnesses of the Negro's fitness to vote and legislate upon the rights of mankind." Delegate Miller continued:

We had built school houses, established charitable institutions, built and maintained the penitentiary system, provided for the education of the deaf and dumb, rebuilt the jails and court houses, rebuilt the bridges and reestablished the ferries. In short, we had reconstructed the State and placed it upon the road to prosperity and, at the same time, by our acts of financial reform transmitted to the Hampton government an indebtedness not greater by more than $2,500,000 than was the bonded debt of the State in 1868, before the Republican Negroes and their white allies came into power.

70

These "imperishable gifts," as delegate Miller described them, were now the exclusive property of whites in South Carolina.

Reconstruction promised much in America, but it left only memories. The Thirteenth, Fourteenth, and Fifteenth Constitutional Amendments that insured black rights were ignored during the years following the overthrow of Reconstruction. The civil rights laws passed in 1866 and 1875 also remained unused. Through their own efforts, blacks continued to make a mark in the South. From 1877 to 1901 five black men were still elected to Congress.

The failures of Reconstruction were an outgrowth of American, not southern, problems. Northerners no more believed in black equality than Southerners. Northerners' devotion to blacks was based on what blacks could do for them. Specifically, they enfranchised blacks so they would vote Republican. Two measures that blacks needed most—education and distribution of the land—the North failed to carry forth. It was not to their interest.

Black voting and other civil rights were granted by law and Constitutional amendments to aid whites in their various causes. As soon as wealthy interests felt that Reconstruction was disturbing business, blacks were handed back to their traditional enemies. Those who really favored black-white governments made up a minority so small, it was hardly identifiable in the nation.

Without land that guaranteed his economic independence, and without the federal government's protection of his rights, the black man was doomed. It was just a matter of time. In some places it took less time than in others. But eventually, it was sealed for all eleven southern states in the bargain that gave the presidential election to Rutherford B. Hayes. On the day of Hayes's election in 1876 as he promised blacks they would be cared for by southern whites, a white mob killed scores of blacks in Hamburg, South Carolina.

The Republican party, despite carrying the Union to victory and passing Reconstruction legislation, cared little for black equality and had never believed in it. For a time it used the black vote to win elections and punish its enemies. But as Middle-West voters increasingly swung to the Republican party, Republicans became less dependent on votes from the South to win future presidential elections. Reconstruction was washed out to sea by the changing needs of northern industrialists and their political spokesmen.

This 1877 cartoon above tries to show that the white man and black man can bury the past and live in peace under white supremacy. Left: violence against blacks did not end with the overthrow of the Reconstruction governments. Murders of blacks by mobs would be common in the southern states for the next fifty years.

*Above: in 1879 thousands of blacks fled the South for Kansas.
Right: the vast majority of blacks failed to obtain any land
through Reconstruction, and after the restoration of white supremacy they still had to labor on fields owned by whites.*

Above: as the black and white governments of the South toppled, people such as this group from Arkansas came to New York seeking a ship that would carry them to Africa. Above left: under white supremacy blacks were again subject to a penal system that jailed them without cause so their labor could be used without pay. Below left: for minor offences, and often for no reason at all, blacks were sentenced to the chain gang.

During Reconstruction blacks, for the first time, were able to secure an education.

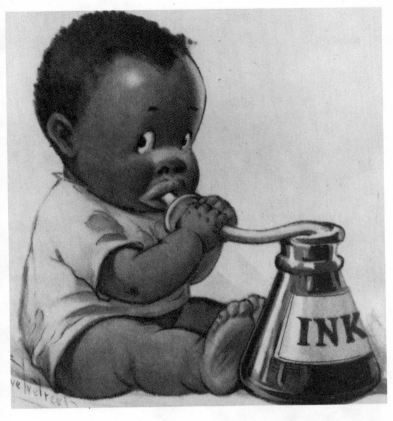

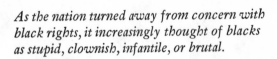

As the nation turned away from concern with black rights, it increasingly thought of blacks as stupid, clownish, infantile, or brutal.

As they looked at the Liberty Bell, this black grandfather and his grandchildren might well have wondered what it meant to their people.

In 1895, when the political cartoon on the previous pages appeared showing the happiness and harmony of free labor in the South, blacks lived under a reign of terror during which almost three black people a week were being lynched. More realistic of what was happening in the country was this cartoon showing the return to Congress of white supremacists who really thought the Confederacy had not been wrong at all; and the situation of these blacks at right who are picking cotton on land owned by whites.

BIBLIOGRAPHY

Bennett, Lerone Jr. *Black Power U.S.A., The Human Side of Reconstruction, 1867–1877.* Chicago: Johnson Publishing Company, Inc., 1967.

Botume, Elizabeth Hyde. *First Days Amongst the Contrabands.* New York: Arno Press and The New York Times, 1968.

Conway, Alan. *The Reconstruction of Georgia.* Minneapolis: University of Minnesota Press, 1965.

Current, Richard N., ed. *Reconstruction [1865–1877].* Englewood Cliffs, New Jersey: Prentice-Hall, Inc., 1965.

Drisko, Carol F. and Toppin,Edgar A. *The Unfinished March.* Garden City, New York: Doubleday & Company, Inc., Zenith Books, 1967.

Du Bois, W. E. B. *Black Reconstruction in Amercia, 1860–1880.* Cleveland, Ohio: The World Publishing Company, 1964.

Franklin, John Hope. *Reconstruction: After the Civil War.* Chicago: The University of Chicago Press, 1961.

King, Edward. *The Great South.* New York: Arno Press and The New York Times, 1969.

Lynch, John R. *The Facts of Reconstruction.* New York: Arno Press and The New York Times, 1968.

Schurz, Carl. *Report on the Condition of the South, 1865.* New York: Arno Press and the New York Times, 1969.

Stampp, Kenneth M. *The Era of Reconstruction, 1865–1877.* New York: Random House, Vintage Books, 1967.

Tindall, George Brown. *South Carolina Negroes, 1877–1900.* Baton Rouge: Louisiana State University Press, 1966.

INDEX

ABOUT THE AUTHOR

═══════

For fifteen years, William Loren Katz has taught United States history to high school students. He has served as a consultant to state departments of education and to the Smithsonian Institution. He has been the Consulting Editor for a series of picture albums on ethnic minority groups in America today, and is the author of *Constitutional Amendments* (A First Book) and *An Album of the Civil War*, all published by Franklin Watts, Inc.

His other works include the award-winning *Eyewitness: The Negro in American History* (1967); *American Majorities and Minorities* (1970); and *The Black West: A Documentary and Pictorial History* (1971). Mr. Katz is presently working on several other books to be published by Franklin Watts, Inc.: *A History of Ethnic Minority Groups in America* (6 volumes); and a study of *Violence in America*. Mr. Katz lives in New York City and was recently a scholar-in-residence at Teachers College, Columbia University.